# THE
# HANDLING

Books are to be returned on or before the last date below.

...ng practical tips
...ng a customer

...nd Anisa

*Published by:*
**Management Pocketbooks Ltd**
Laurel House, Station Approach, Alresford, Hants SO24 9JH, U.K.
Tel: +44 (0)1962 735573   Fax: +44 (0)1962 733637
E-mail: sales@pocketbook.co.uk
Website: www.pocketbook.co.uk

This edition published 2001.   Reprinted 2003, 2004, 2007.

© Angelena Boden 2001.

ISBN  978 1 870471 91 6

Design, Typeset & Graphics by **efex Ltd**.      Printed in U.K.

# CONTENTS

# THE SAD TALE OF 'BLOOMING FLOWERS'

'Blooming Flowers' was a well established garden centre on the outskirts of a growing town. Two years before it closed it had expanded to include a café, a gift shop and an organic fruit and vegetable outlet. As well as employing a core staff of ten it took on a number of seasonal and part-time staff. The company didn't have a customer service policy nor did it believe in 'wasting' money on training. Customers seemed happy enough. After all they hardly got any complaints. No, 'everything in the garden was rosy'.

The manager should have been a bit suspicious. No complaints doesn't mean that all customers are happy. Most of us don't bother complaining. We just walk away and don't go back.

HELLO, CAN I SPEAK TO THE MANAGER PLEASE!

1

# THE SAD TALE OF 'BLOOMING FLOWERS'

The expansion, unsurprisingly, led to a variety of organisational and logistical problems. There were staffing shortages, managerial inexperience, reduction in quality. Gradually business dropped off but still nothing was done about it.

The staff stopped telling the manager about some of the problems they had encountered because he wouldn't listen. He spent a lot of money on advertising, and making big capital changes. He never once thought of getting some feedback from the customers. Eventually the inevitable happened.  The business had to close.

Businesses need complaints. You will read this more than once in this book!

Complaints point out where we need to improve and help us to build on customer satisfaction. Many people don't like handling complaints. They feel they don't have the knowledge or are frightened of people who get angry. This Pocketbook will help you identify the different ways in which people complain, understand why and give you some tips on how to handle them.

It can be a great source of job satisfaction when you turn a grizzly bear into a Cheshire cat!

# WHY PEOPLE COMPLAIN

## UNDERSTANDING WHY

It is said that 91% of people don't complain. They prefer to get their revenge by not buying from a business that has given them an inferior product or a poor service. More dangerous is the statistic that every dissatisfied customer shares their bad experience with another seven people.

They have a passive power and they know it!

We complain for very different reasons, not all of them genuine ones, yet you need to treat each complaint on its merits.

Knowing why people complain can help with the way you respond. You can identify those who are upset and show empathy. Chronic complainers or those who do it for the sake of it need firmer handling. As for professional complainers, who are out to seek compensation or intimidate with threats of legal action, you need to be particularly careful about what you say and refer them on to someone more senior if necessary.

# WHY PEOPLE COMPLAIN

## REASONS

While there are many reasons for making a complaint, it is difficult to determine what percentage of people fall into each category. Often their reasons are multiple.

Whatever the reason for dissatisfaction you should never underestimate the feelings that lie behind it. All complainers need handling with a good listening ear, understanding, tact and carefully chosen words. What might seem innocuous at first could turn into something complex and unpleasant. Don't take anything for granted.

# REASONS

## QUALITY OF PRODUCT

A sub-standard product which doesn't live up to its claims is a major source of complaint.

The product might:

- Be of inferior material to what was expected
- Be poorly finished off
- Have too much 'padding' making it deceptively larger
- Have a short lifespan
- Be of limited potential
- Have a faulty design (potentially dangerous)

If customers believe they have been misled, they feel angry and want to take further action.

# WHY PEOPLE COMPLAIN

## REASONS
### QUALITY OF SERVICE

Today's customers are more demanding and have a greater awareness of what good service should be. (How many times have you heard someone say: 'The Americans know how to look after people'?)

We all want to be treated as if we matter and our business is as important as the next person's.

We will complain about:

- Indifferent attitudes
- Lack of manners – downright rudeness
- More concern with profit than people
- Slow responses
- Poor product knowledge on the part of the staff
- Lack of communication skills

# REASONS

## EXPECTATIONS NOT BEING MET

There are three stages leading up to a purchase:

1. **Anticipation** - savouring the idea of the purchase; reading the information
2. **Planning** - deciding where/when to go, with whom, how much to spend
3. **Discussion** - involving others in the decision-making process

These mental processes make us anxious and/or excited, and have our expectations running high. We are finely tuned to possible faults and can be quick to criticise. After all, we are spending our money.

The gap between **reality** and **fantasy** can grow very wide.

For some people nothing is ever quite enough. We sometimes believe that by buying a new hi-fi, car, holiday or kitchen we are going to solve our problems and feel happier. Spending money is often a quick fix; if the purchase doesn't do 'its job' we feel justified in making a complaint.

## WHY PEOPLE COMPLAIN

# REASONS

## BECAUSE WE CAN!

Thanks to consumer watchdog programmes and various customer charters telling us what to do if we are not happy with a product/service, we are much better informed about our rights. Thinking we might get compensation as well as a replacement is a good enough motive to encourage complaints (even if we have to fabricate a little bit).

However, when we do complain we find it's not always as straightforward as it first appears.

Take, for example, a complaint made about train delays.

Firstly, the train has to be delayed by a certain length of time.
Secondly, your ticket has to be stamped to prove you were on that delayed train.
Thirdly, you have to complete and return a form.
Lastly, you will only receive a percentage of your ticket price – after all you did make the journey!

# REASONS
## TO BE DIFFICULT

Some people are just natural complainers. They want to make life as complicated as possible not only for themselves but for others. They seem to harbour a sense of permanent outrage, that shows itself in a number of ways including fault-finding.

Trying to pacify and please these perverse characters can prove to be frustrating and unrewarding. The secret is not to allow them to attack and blame you personally.

Difficult people come in three main varieties: **angry and aggressive, silent and menacing, obstinate and argumentative.**

# REASONS

## IT'S THEIR JOB

It is estimated that 2% of people who complain do so for a living. They are the **professional** complainers. They are very well informed via the media, they know their rights and they have the communication skills of a good lawyer.

They often prey on new businesses, particularly restaurants and, having planned their strategy well in advance, will use their knowledge of the law, quoting chapter and verse. They like to name drop 'My solicitor plays golf with your MD' and will have first class product knowledge.

It is best to let the experienced staff in your organisation handle these manipulators, as one false word can land you in court.

# REASONS
## TO BE HELPFUL!

Some customers believe they are doing you a favour (and of course they are - see Chapter 2). They have great ideas about how you could improve your systems, your product and your service. What they don't take into account is the chance that you might have tried all this before, or that their suggestions are much too costly.

'This is such a cosy teashop. I love the log fire and the classical music. If you offered cucumber sandwiches it would be perfect.'

These are the **constructive** complainers but, as we shall see, there is often a hidden agenda behind their good intentions.

# WHY PEOPLE COMPLAIN

## REASONS
### FROM BOREDOM

People who do not lead rewarding and fulfilling lives, or who find communication with other people difficult, are often bored and miserable and look for ways to get excitement. Instead of taking up a sport or hobby, they find pleasure in winding other people up. Those of you working in customer service positions are prime targets for such game playing.

Others do it out of a sense of feeling **entitled**. *I was promised the best, I deserve the best and I shall make sure you give me the best, even if I am not prepared to pay for it, because I have always had it.*

# NOTES

# WELCOMING COMPLAINTS

# WHY COMPLAINTS ARE GOOD NEWS

*We love getting complaints!*

*We need to get complaints!*

*Let's encourage our customers to complain!*

Can you relate to this? Perhaps you prefer to keep your fingers crossed and hope that customers will smile sweetly and sigh, 'Oh well, never mind. We all make mistakes'.

Complaints are to be welcomed because they provide direction towards making improvements.

COMPLAINT → IMPROVEMENTS → SATISFIED CUSTOMERS → **IMPROVED BUSINESS**

# COMPLAINTS ARE OPPORTUNITIES!

Opportunities to do what?

- Evaluate how well you are doing
- Identify weak points in your systems and processes and put them right
- See situations from the customer's point of view
- Improve customer satisfaction
- Create long-term loyalty – handling disgruntled customers well often leaves them feeling more positive about your organisation than before

# SOME SCARY FACTS

One unhappy customer tells 10 to15 others about their bad experience. If it's really bad they'll tell the whole world.

For every complaint that could be made, around 20 people don't bother. This means 20 lost opportunities.

If you handle a complaint badly or with a 'couldn't care less' attitude or, worse still, if you hide behind the 'rule book', you will lose that customer for good.

You can't afford to lose even 50p because this will mount up according to something known as the multiplier effect.

# THE INCOME MULTIPLIER EFFECT

**Example**

A customer comes into a leisure centre which was built last year. The centre is trying to build up its customer base. It employs 50 staff, part time and full time, who haven't received much training in customer service and complaint handling.

The customer asks about booking a squash court for later that day. He doesn't get a positive reply and the receptionist's attitude is very much 'take it or leave it'. He shrugs and walks away.

How much has the centre lost in potential revenue?

- **£5.00** primary spend – the price of a squash court
- **£5.00** secondary spend – a drink, sandwich, possibly a swim, etc
- **£500.00** potential membership fees

He will tell at least **seven** people about his bad experience so  **£510 x 7 = £ 3,570.**

It is easy for a small amount of lost income to multiply to dangerous proportions.

# MAKE IT EASY TO COMPLAIN

Customers may well want to tell you they're unhappy about something but they either:

- Feel uncomfortable about doing so
- Don't know how to
- Don't have time; it's easier to let it go

So, give them a choice of mechanisms. For example:

- Simple questionnaires with pre-paid postage
- Telephone help line
- Customer service points
- Exit surveys – face to face questions
- Comment cards

Offer some incentives – prize draws, special offers, free gifts.

# MAKE IT EASY TO COMPLAIN

Let them know it's not a waste of time!

What are you going to do with the information? File it away? Shred it for next year's Christmas decorations?

One company in Birmingham maintains a whiteboard in the reception listing the key comments/complaints made by customers, with a note of the action taken, or to be taken, and by whom. Customers really feel they are part of the product and service improvement team.

Customers need to know what's in it for them if they do complain.

*Full refund within 14 days*
*Immediate replacement – no quibble*

Respond quickly to complaints. If you give a number to ring, make sure someone is always there to answer the phone. Reply within two days if that's what you have promised to do.

# BE NICE!

There's no point setting up a complaints system if the people servicing it don't want to be there, hate dealing with problems and have a bad attitude.

One way to get on the right side of a furious customer is to

**USE YOUR EARS AND YOUR EYES**

and **NOT YOUR MOUTH.**

# TIPS ON BEING NICE

- Smile (not a cheesy grin; that will wind people up)
- Make eye contact – don't stare, glare, roll your eyes, or flirt
- Use a friendly, polite greeting
- Keep your voice calm
- Be cheerful, but not irritatingly so
- Make sure your systems are customer friendly (all the smiling in the world won't help matters if you have to tell customers they can't have their order for Christmas)
- Own up to mistakes – don't deny or be defensive (showing your human side is your best asset)

# REDUCING COMPLAINTS

It might sound a bit of a paradox, but welcoming complaints can reduce complaints.

# CUSTOMER FEEDBACK

Keep asking your customers what more they would like from you. If they want home delivery, work on that. Carry out a feasibility study. Make sure your system works, but **don't** promise anything you can't deliver, or have to withdraw at a later stage because of inadequate research.

**Be ahead of your competitors.
Keep offering added value to your product.**

NOTES

# HOW PEOPLE COMPLAIN

# EMOTIONS RUN HIGH

In an ideal world all customers, and that includes you and me, would voice their complaints clearly, politely and with consideration towards the feelings of others.

The reality is that the customer doesn't care about anything other than getting a speedy and satisfactory conclusion to the problem. They'll shout, swear, threaten, play mind games, suggest they introduce you to their solicitor …

In fact, even the most pleasant people can become irrational if they believe they have been cheated in some way.

Perhaps the easiest way of dealing with a complaint is face to face, yet more and more people are choosing to vent their feelings by telephone, letter or e-mail. As internet shopping becomes more widely available, and the preferred method for many, it is more convenient to bash out an e-mail while anger is still fresh!

Let's look at some of the typical types of complainer businesses have to face.

# AGGRESSIVE COMPLAINERS

When we think of complaints we often think of aggression. Many people do feel they have to become angry to be taken seriously and to be believed. For them attack is the best form of defence. Anger gives them a feeling of being in control rather than at your mercy.

Aggression is also a visible expression of frustration. Customers using this approach do so because it is all they know. They want to intimidate you and appear more powerful than they feel. To understand more about the psychology of behaviours read my book *The Problem Behaviour Pocketbook*.

# AGGRESSIVE COMPLAINERS

What aggressive complainers need from you is:

- Someone to take notice
- Appreciation of just how angry they are
- Permission to let off steam
- A feeling of being back in control
- Explanations not excuses
- A solution

What they don't want from you is:

- To be patronised
- To be denied their feelings
- Shouting back
- An argument
- Denial and justification
- Authoritative behaviour

# AGGRESSIVE COMPLAINERS

## WHAT SHOULD YOU DO?

There are two key issues to consider when dealing with any kind of complaint:

a) understanding the feelings behind it

b) dealing with the practicalities of finding a solution

### Feelings

Anger is frightening but it is often a mask for fear and anxiety. The following actions should help:

- Calm the person down – give them some space, talk quietly, be calm yourself
- Don't become hostile or defensive
- Try to look beyond the rudeness
- Stay focused on the problem
- Show the customer you are taking the matter seriously and that you are pleased they have taken the trouble to talk to you
- Move them away from other customers if they are shouting or being abusive; anger is infectious

# AGGRESSIVE COMPLAINERS

## WHAT SHOULD YOU DO?

**Facts**

- Establish the facts of the problem
- Involve the customer – 'What would you like us to do?'
- Discuss alternatives if necessary
- Arrive at an agreement
- Take action
- Follow up the action to make sure promises are being delivered

**Tips**

- Don't take it personally
- Find out what sort of history the customer has with you and whether there have been problems before
- Use the person's name – it's good customer service – but don't overdo it

# AGGRESSIVE COMPLAINERS

## WHAT SHOULD YOU DO?

### Taking an angry phone call

You may not be dealing with your customer face to face. On the telephone, you only have your ears and your mouth, so use them to good advantage: 80% ears: 20% mouth (or less)!

- Listen actively – give feedback to show you haven't nodded off
- Keep your voice even – use a calm, controlled tone of voice
- Don't be tempted to attack, patronise or deny because you are talking to a disembodied voice
- Don't roll your eyes, sigh or drum your fingers, they'll pick up on it somehow
- Don't put the phone down in exasperation

### Replying to an angry e-mail or letter

- Put it on one side for a few hours – let your temper cool
- Stick to the facts
- Don't reply with inflammatory language
- Be very polite and considered
- Ask someone to check your reply before it is sent

# PASSIVE COMPLAINERS

**Passive complainers** take two forms:

**Type A**
They don't say anything; they simply don't return and they pass on the bad news to others. These make up the majority.

**Type B**
A minority of people who are dangerous because their aggression is covert. They use mind games to get their point across and make poisonous little barbs when you are least expecting them.

When asked if everything is to their satisfaction, they will smile and say, 'Yes thank you', then will add, 'There is just one thing …'. This unleashes a steady stream of complaints said so sweetly you can't decide whether or not they are serious.

They are. Deadly.

# HOW PEOPLE COMPLAIN

## PASSIVE COMPLAINERS

### TYPE A

With **Type A** you need to be able to read the non-verbal signals:

- Frowning
- Tight lipped expression
- Reduced eye contact
- Detached manner

Create an opportunity to ask open questions:

'How did you find the new washing powder?'

Not 'Was the new washing powder alright?'

The latter will only get a *yes* or *no* answer.

Be open yourself. Let them see that you welcome complaints. If they prefer to put something in writing make it easy for them to do so. Above all, don't let them store it all up. Who knows what stories they might tell others.

# PASSIVE COMPLAINERS

## TYPE B

**Type B** need more careful handling:

- Don't be intimidated by the silence; keep asking open questions
- Don't show any signs of frustration, despair or weakening; that's just what they want
- Don't react to the throw-away remarks or sarcastic one-liners – these are designed to throw you off course
- Stick to the facts and keep bringing **them** back to the facts

These people are hard work. They are unreasonable, awkward, and will deliberately and convincingly argue that black is white (you end up believing it!). They can be very nasty and play on your sense of fear.

Be ready for them.

# CONSTRUCTIVE COMPLAINERS

Some customers feel they could run your business better than you do. They are full of useful ideas for change. On the surface it seems as if they want to help but this is just another way of expressing their dissatisfaction. They don't want a head-on confrontation but want you to read between the lines.

- Don't dismiss their ideas
- Thank them for their suggestions
- Put right what you can
- Don't say anything that might sound like a promise: 'When you come back ...'

# PROFESSIONAL COMPLAINERS

Clever, cunning, expert at convincing you that you are wrong. They use a whole bag of tricks.

- *I play golf with your Chairman*
- *My solicitor is your MD's cousin*
- *I worked for 30 years in this business. I do know what I am talking about.*

- *The law states …*
- *I know my rights …*

You can spot a professional complainer, ie: someone who does it for a living, or who is out to get compensation, by their self assurance, their in-depth product knowledge and their manner of speech. It's often a gut instinct.

What do you do?
- Sit tight; don't be intimidated
- Listen and make notes. This might throw them off balance
- Don't show any signs of nervousness
- Stick closely to procedures
- Treat their complaint the same way you would treat any other
- Call a superior if you need to

# DEVELOPING A POLICY

DEVELOPING A POLICY

# CONSISTENT APPROACH

Most medium to large businesses have a policy for handling complaints but perhaps need to review it from time to time. Businesses that take a more *ad hoc* line would benefit from developing a consistent approach. Whatever policy is in place it should be:

- Easy to understand
- Simple to implement
- Effectively communicated to all staff

## DEVELOPING A POLICY

# WHAT TO INCLUDE

Some of the key features of a good policy include:

- Mechanisms for people to complain
- System for logging and analysing complaints
- Identification of those who will be responsible
- Procedures for handling different levels of complaint
- Ways of keeping customers informed
- Structure of compensations
- Follow-up action

# INFORMATION FROM CUSTOMERS

There is no point having a policy to handle unhappy customers if they are not encouraged to come forward in the first place. Such an invitation to comment or complain can take the form of something impersonal written on the packaging:

*Customers who are not entirely satisfied with this product should ... (action)*

Or something very personal, following the example of the Chairman of Pret à Manger food chain who prints his own phone number on the packaging of products!

Questionnaires, comment cards, suggestion boxes, exit surveys, market research are all positive ways of encouraging customer feedback.

Informal verbal feedback from talking to customers is often the most valuable of all!

# LOGGING & ANALYSING COMPLAINTS

It is essential to have a system in place that collates and considers the nature of a complaint if corrective action is to be taken to prevent a re-occurrence.

To do this it is important to **define** what your company means by a complaint.

- Is it solely when someone gets angry?
- Is it when they mildly point out an error?
- Is it when they are deliberately trying to be awkward?

Not everything that goes wrong warrants a complaint, eg: a certain number of faults with machinery is to be expected.

# DEVELOPING A POLICY

## LOGGING

Consider what kind of information you need:

- Name, address, contact numbers
- Date, nature of complaint
- Action – solution suggested
- Customer response to suggestion
- Time-frame to put matters right
- Person responsible for action
- Corrective action to be taken to prevent problem from recurring

A computerised database is the most obvious way of recording and storing information, but paper back-up systems can prove to be a godsend!

# ANALYSING

Analysis will throw up recurring problems and weak areas, and identify particular periods or departments involved. All information needs to be presented in a simple, non-critical fashion and passed to the relevant managers. They in turn will need to consult staff and formulate corrective action.

Switched-on managers and directors will want periodic information about customer complaints. Some companies attach bonuses and other rewards to the fall in numbers of complaints received.

DEVELOPING A POLICY

# WHO DEALS WITH THE COMPLAINT?

## CUSTOMER SERVICE DESKS

Identifying key people in the organisation to deal specifically with customer complaints, comments and even compliments has become a preferred approach for major retailers and transport companies. Staff need to be highly trained to handle all kinds of difficult people and situations, and need full support from the rest of the team and the management.

- Customer Service desks become central points easily identified and accessible by consumers
- Smaller businesses may identify individuals in each department to do a similar job
- Some managers prefer all staff to be able to deal effectively with complaints whether or not it is anything to do with them

Whatever the approach adopted, the system must be clearly identified and communicated to everyone. The bottom line is that the customer doesn't care who deals with the problem as long as someone does!

# ESTABLISHING PROCEDURES

Complaints will fit (not always neatly) into different categories and levels, all requiring specific handling. However, some basic ground rules need to be established:

- Acknowledge the customer's grievance
- Make eye contact – don't look defensive
- Listen carefully, make notes, give feedback
- Empathise with their feelings
- Don't patronise when you apologise
- Discuss solutions and corrective action
- Agree action depending on your level of empowerment
- Follow-up: 'Did you sort it out?'

# TECHNIQUES FOR SPECIAL SITUATIONS

### The manipulator

Everyone would like something for nothing given the chance, but most of us stop short of deliberate scheming. Those who are clearly out to complain to get freebies – meals, vouchers, tickets – need **firm** handling otherwise they go away and tell their friends to try the same trick. They could put you out of business.

### The noisy one

Plenty of volume, fist thumping, table banging, bulging veins but no real cause for complaint. Sounds familiar?

These people just want to be heard. They've got a bit of a chip on their shoulder. Take them away from the crowd, sit them down (it's harder to get angry then), stay in control and if all else fails say, 'I'm not prepared to listen until you stop shouting'. If need be, call for back-up.

# TECHNIQUES FOR SPECIAL SITUATIONS

### Chronic complainers

Some people (less than 10%) complain out of habit. It's a behaviour pattern they have learned. You can see them coming, again and again.

Be patient, don't give them real cause to complain about your attitude.
Ask closed questions, keep dialogue to a minimum.
Stick to the point.

Some managers call their bluff.

'Well, Mr. Smythe. I am really sorry you are yet again unhappy with our service. Perhaps you would like to try … on Blob Street.'

This often stops them in their tracks.

# DRAWING THE LINE

Every company will draw its own boundaries but some general guidelines used by many businesses include:

- Threats of violence – physical and verbal
- Abuse – swearing, shouting
- When **nothing** seems to be acceptable
- When reason doesn't prevail
- When you correct the problem but then there's something else …!
- When it's clear your customer is out to abuse the system

Some customers aren't worth having.
They are **bad** for business.
Don't be frightened about losing them.

# COMMUNICATING
# WITH THE COMPLAINER

# COMMUNICATION SKILLS

Handling any sort of conflict requires you to draw on all your resources. In particular, you need to have a good rummage in your communication tool box! We all have many communication skills but don't always use them effectively.

We relate to people on two levels:

**Consciously:** when we CHOOSE our words, gestures and behaviours.

**Subconsciously:** when unknowingly we send out SUBLIMINAL messages. These often have the most impact on people and can make them feel uncomfortable.

## COMMUNICATING WITH THE COMPLAINER

# LISTENING SKILLS

There are two aspects to communicating: receiving and sending messages.

Would you say you are a good listener? Consider the following questions:

- Do you have a tendency to interrupt or finish off customers' sentences for them?
- Do you find yourself losing patience or concentration?

If so, you need to work on your listening skills. Or:

- Do you stay focused on your customers?
- Do you make notes, give good feedback and demonstrate that they have your full attention?

Showing customers you are listening by nodding and asking questions is a good way of demonstrating that you are taking them seriously.

# COMMUNICATING WITH THE COMPLAINER

## LISTENING SKILLS

Listening, however, is a difficult task for most people. It requires you to:

- Block out all distractions
- Be observant – use eyes and ears more than mouth!
- Keep an open mind and not be judgemental
- Stay calm, not rising to any bait
- Keep all personal prejudices at bay
- Listen all the way through
- Read between the lines – is there something the customer is not telling you?

## COMMUNICATING WITH THE COMPLAINER

# LANGUAGE

In difficult situations most people are careful to choose their words by avoiding:

- Inflammatory language, eg: *That's a ridiculous thing to say*

- Criticism, eg: *You should have contacted … dept*

- Swearing, eg: *!!\*\*?\*!!*

- Insensitive language, eg: *It's not designed for people over xxx stone*

- Negativity, eg: *It's not possible*

- Overbearing, eg: *It MUST reach us by…*

# NON-VERBAL LANGUAGE

Inappropriate words can hurt or incite anger in another. However, it is not the most powerful form of communication. According to the experts the breakdown is as follows:

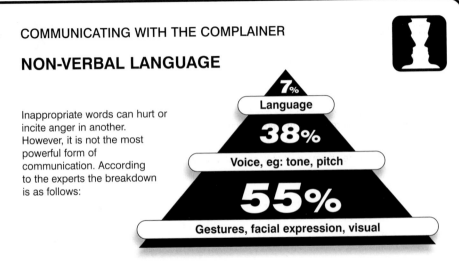

**7%**
Language

**38%**
Voice, eg: tone, pitch

**55%**
Gestures, facial expression, visual

This is particularly true of communication relating to emotion. Positive language delivered in an abrasive or monotonous voice will have a negative impact. We're more aware of *how* people say things than *what* they say.

# BODY LANGUAGE

Body language is understood by most people in business today. Inappropriate facial expressions, posture, sharp movements can make a situation much worse.

'There's no need to look at me like that!' (said the customer).

As a brief reminder, if you want to keep your unhappy customer calm, avoid:

- Putting up barriers – folded arms, glaring, hiding behind folders or a desk

- Aggressive gestures – finger pointing, posturing, hands on hips, feet apart

- Showing you are bored or irritated – foot tapping, sighing, looking at the clock

Stay relaxed, use open gestures, make good but not excessive eye contact.

Even when you are talking on the telephone, these gestures can communicate through your voice. Be careful.

57

# COMMUNICATING WITH THE COMPLAINER

## STAYING POSITIVE

Why is a positive style of communication helpful?

- It helps to keep everyone calm, including you

- Taking control of your actions gives you time to think, observe and stay objective

- It helps to prevent the situation from becoming worse, which would only give the customer something else to complain about

- It helps to counteract aggression – it's difficult to shout at someone who is calm and controlled

- You are continuing to act in a professional manner on behalf of the organisation, no matter how you might *feel* about the situation and the customer

COMMUNICATING WITH THE COMPLAINER

# TELEPHONE COMMUNICATION SKILLS

One of the biggest disadvantages when trying to sort out a complaint from an angry customer over the telephone is the heavy reliance on language and voice. The phone is a sensitive instrument and people pick up on sighs and irritation. They also know whether or not you are eating, drinking or smoking. But they can't see your face and have no idea whether or not you are taking them seriously.

You can:

- Smile into the phone – it makes you sound friendly and caring

- Give plenty of verbal feedback to let them know you are listening; it's no good nodding unless you have a video phone!

- Paraphrase and summarise to ensure you have fully understood

- Press the silent button if you need to confer with someone in the office; no one likes to hear themselves being talked about

- Try to create an atmosphere of trust and sincerity – they need to know you're not just saying anything to get rid of them

# WRITTEN COMMUNICATION

When you only have words to play with, you have to make them work for you.

Whether you are writing a letter, sending an e-mail or even a text message by phone, attention to detail is essential.

You never know who is going to see your written communication. It can always be used as evidence so you need to be **clear, concise and correct.**

Presentation speaks volumes and will go a long way to portraying the sort of company you are. Spelling, syntax, positioning of words all count.

Most importantly, make it a rule to reply **as quickly as possible.** Customers want a speedy response, at least, to their problem even if it takes a bit of time to sort out the solution. Days, even weeks, of silence will just make them more frustrated!

# THE PSYCHOLOGY OF COMMUNICATION

# THE PSYCHOLOGY OF COMMUNICATION

## TRANSACTIONAL ANALYSIS

Much of our communication is unconscious. We don't actively decide what quality of eye contact we should use or consider the impact of our words on other people and the consequences.

When you watch someone's facial expression change or sense a shift in mood it becomes obvious that there has been a deep reaction to the communication 'stimulus'.

The study of such responses is called Transactional Analysis, developed by Dr. Eric Berne, an American psychiatrist in the 1950s.

Transactional Analysis :

- Is an analytical thinking process
- Provides insight
- Gives control over actions and reactions

# TRANSACTIONAL ANALYSIS

Knowing the basics about Transactional Analysis will give you a better understanding of **why** people communicate in a certain way. For example, why they feel the need to be aggressive or manipulative to get their point across when they are unhappy about something.

A child who has had to shout to make his parents listen to him will often take this communication pattern into adult life. He will shout at **you** because he is conditioned to think **you** won't listen either.

It will also help you choose a more appropriate style of communication with which to respond.

# THE PSYCHOLOGY OF COMMUNICATION

## EGO STATES

Berne became aware that within each individual there exist three personalities or **ego states** which have their own ways of communicating and behaving. He also discovered that we shift from one state to another subconsciously. These states are not 'roles' but psychological realities which are activated by feelings.

He identified them as Parent, Adult and Child ego states. Transactional Analysis is sometimes called PAC communication.

These personalities develop in the first few years of life and will be shaped according to background, experiences and upbringing.

THE PSYCHOLOGY OF COMMUNICATION

# EGO STATE MODEL

***NP:*** Nurturing Parent
***CP:*** Controlling Parent

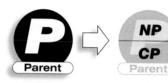

- Logical
- Detached
- Unemotional
- 'Data Processing'

***FC:*** Free Child
***AC:*** Adapted Child

# THE PSYCHOLOGY OF COMMUNICATION

## EGO STATES

### PARENT

Imagine a tape recorder being switched on at birth and all thoughts, feelings, events and behaviours recorded in an unedited version.

The Parent ego state develops by recording all the 'rules and laws' of the household, characterised by *'No'*, *'Don't'*, *frowning, finger wagging, routines, attitudes, value laden standards, prejudices, criticisms.*

There is also another side to the Parent: the nurturing, caring, gentle controlling side.

In later life memories of these behaviours are triggered and *parent responses* copied.

Think of all the behaviours, body language, facial expressions, attitudes you have taken from your parent (substitute). Has anyone said, 'You're just like your mother' or 'Like father, like son'?

# THE PSYCHOLOGY OF COMMUNICATION

## EGO STATES

CHILD

At the same time another recording is being made which is the internalising of the response to the Parent behaviours (how the Child feels about them).

Cross looks, sharp words, a smack, neglect, sarcasm can only be recorded as feelings in the child.

**Negative Parent Behaviours** 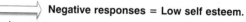 **Negative responses = Low self esteem.**

Soon the child either learns to seek parent approval, giving up pleasurable exploration of the world and becoming the *Adapted Child,* or rebels.

The child also stores much positive data: fun times, discovery, creativity, carefree activity, eg: puddle jumping.

Think of behaviours you still use from your childhood when bad feelings are triggered; door slamming, sulking, temper tantrums, not speaking. Our Child state can take over inappropriately if we let it.

Think about the complainers you have dealt with recently. Have you noticed similar behaviours?

# THE PSYCHOLOGY OF COMMUNICATION

## EGO STATES

### ADULT

Once a child learns to move about he or she acquires some independence and control. He/she finds out things independently and collects data and learns to work out his/her own understanding of life. This is the Adult ego state beginning to form.

The Adult is described as a data-processing computer which makes decisions based on *logic and factual information and is not influenced by feelings*. It analyses the data in the Parent and accepts it or rejects it, and considers the feelings stirred in the Child for appropriateness. It carries out probability estimating, eg: in a complaint situation *'How likely is it that I am going to get this sorted out?'*.

It can also devise solutions, develop contingency plans and accept the inevitable with equanimity.

# THE PSYCHOLOGY OF COMMUNICATION

## PARENT COMPLAINER

How are these ego states activated when people are dissatisfied customers?

Customers who complain from their Parent draw on criticism, challenging attitudes and an authoritative position (from their personal database). They will use a range of verbal, vocal and non-verbal behaviours.

Their non-verbal and verbal indicators will be:

- Head shaking, arms folded, tongue clicking
- *I paid good money for this*
- *It's a disgrace*
- *I'm going to report you to …*

They approach the situation from a position of 'How dare they … !'.

# THE PSYCHOLOGY OF COMMUNICATION

## CHILD COMPLAINER

The Child is activated when strong feelings of being ignored, cheated or controlled are triggered. In this ego state we often feel either powerless or rebellious.

Many of the clues to show someone is operating from their Child include: temper tantrums, sulking, nail-biting, no eye contact, nervous laughter, throat clearing.

Indicators will be:

- *It's not fair*
- *Why should I?*
- *I'm not moving from here until I get a replacement*

# THE PSYCHOLOGY OF COMMUNICATION

## ADULT COMPLAINER

The Adult will be activated once the attitudes and feelings of the Parent and Child have been analysed for their usefulness and put aside.

It will ask questions, make comparisons, stay objective, not be opinionated, seek out the facts. It does not send subliminal messages, has no hidden agenda and does not play mind games.

The customer who complains from the Adult will have acknowledged feelings of anger but has not allowed them to take over. He/she wants a practical solution to the problem and not to indulge in psychological warfare in order to feel better (ie: a replay of a childhood battle).

# THE PSYCHOLOGY OF COMMUNICATION

## EGO STATES

### SUMMARY

When you are in your Parent ego state you use words, behaviours and actions of your parent (substitute).

**We all carry our Parent inside**

When your Child is showing you are replaying behaviours and reactions you would have used as a small child.

**Our Child can always be activated under certain conditions**

Operating from your Adult means you have made an objective, logical, autonomous appraisal of the situation.

**We are all capable of objectivity**

We don't have to be the victims of our childhood behaviour patterns. We have a choice. In business communication we can only safely operate from our Adult.

# ANALYSING THE
## <u>TRANSACTIONS</u>

# ANALYSING THE TRANSACTIONS

## STIMULUS & RESPONSE

Put two people together and eventually they will communicate, either with language or gestures. Whoever sends the first message is sending the transaction **stimulus.**
The other person will do something to relate to this stimulus. This is the transactional **response.**

Simple transactional analysis is concerned with diagnosing which **ego state** implemented the stimulus and which executed the response.

The simplest of transactions are **Adult to Adult.**

'I'd like to exchange these shoes, please.'
(factual request – no emotion)

'Would you tell me what's wrong with them?'
(factual response – no old wounds triggered)

**STIMULUS**   **RESPONSE**

# STIMULUS & RESPONSE

This is a **Complimentary Transaction**, ie: when the response is appropriate and falls within the natural order of human relationships.

Transactions proceed in chains so that each response also becomes a stimulus. Communication will proceed smoothly while transactions remain complimentary.

There are other forms of complimentary transactions, ie: Parent to Parent, Child to Child, but they carry risks.

Adult to Adult transactions draw on logic and not emotions. If customers were to complain from their Adult state it would be easier to solve their problems.

# CROSSED TRANSACTIONS

When communication breaks down it is usually as a result of crossed transactions – which are emotionally loaded. The most common crossed transaction is the following:

**Stimulus:** Adult (hoping to hook Adult response)

'Your conditions of service state that delivery will be in 14 days. It is 24 days since I ordered. Would you please explain.'

The appropriate Adult response would be:

'Yes, delivery should be within 14 days. The reason for the delay is … I'm sorry but I will make sure … Let me have your order number …'

# CROSSED TRANSACTIONS

However this may be **heard** as a Parent criticism because there is a transference reaction. Then the response is triggered from the Child.

The response would be:

'You'll have to speak to X in despatch. I don't deal with …'
(This is the rebellious Child hitting back at the Parent: *Don't blame me again*)

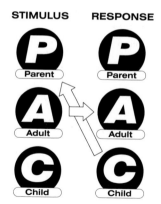

STIMULUS     RESPONSE

77

# CROSSED TRANSACTIONS

Crossed transactions occur as a result of reading into comments messages that are not there. This can lead to an impasse and a series of fiery exchanges. Many people fall naturally into a groove of crossed transactions and go on the defensive.

Crossed transactions occur between customers and suppliers, managers and workforce, between colleagues, in fact in any communication situation.

Further example:

'My telephone bill is incorrect.' ( Adult)
'Why haven't you rung accounts? This is sales.'
(Critical Parent)

This will lead to further inappropriate exchanges until the original subject is lost.

# UNCROSSING A TRANSACTION

The crossed transaction does not always come from the response. It can be triggered in the first stimulus.

'What do you call this? (pointing to a cloudy pint of beer). It's disgraceful!'
(Parent trying to trigger Child)

If the response is Adult the crossed transaction can be stopped in its tracks.

'I'm sorry, sir. Let me change it for you.' (Adult)

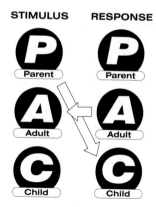

# UNCROSSING TRANSACTIONS

Using an Adult response is an essential approach when dealing with complaints voiced from the Parent or Child ego states which are expressing life positions.

For example:
'It's not fair.' (Child)
'It's a disgrace.' (Parent)

Recognise the ego state of the complainant:

- Don't get 'hooked'
- Remember you and they have a choice (Parent/Adult/Child)
- Watch out for signs that the ego state is shifting
- Stay in Adult at all times

# ULTERIOR TRANSACTIONS

More complex are **ulterior transactions.** These involve two or more ego states simultaneously.

'They (cakes) look nice.' (Adult)

*Ulterior transaction: 'I would like one.' (Child)*

'They do, don't they?' (Adult)

*Ulterior transaction: 'You're not having one.' (Parent)*

Sales people are clever at using ulterior transactions.

'This hi-fi is better but more expensive.' (Adult)

*Ulterior transaction: You probably can't afford it. (Parent)*

'I'll take it.' (Adult)

*'I'll show you, you arrogant....' (Child)*

**STIMULUS**  **RESPONSE**

Parent

Parent

Adult

Adult

Child

Child

81

# STAYING IN ADULT

- Be tuned into Parent and Child feelings and responses
- Avoid externalising your feelings
- Count to 10 to delay the automatic triggered response
- Compute appropriate responses
- Don't say it if you're unsure of the impact it will have
- Don't let others trigger your Parent/Child.

You always have a **choice.**

You should choose Adult when dealing with complaints. It is the only way to minimise damage, get the matter sorted out quickly and restore the customer's confidence.

# ANALYSING THE TRANSACTIONS

## SUMMARY

An understanding of Transactional Analysis is useful in all types of business communication but particularly when dealing with dissatisfied customers, clients and difficult colleagues.

- It provides an analytical insight into what lies behind the communication process
- You can consciously choose your ego state
- It should help you to deal with complaints in a constructive and non-personal manner

For further reading see the Bibliography at the end of the book.

# NOTES

# INTERNAL COMPLAINTS

# DEFINING THE CUSTOMER

Ask a colleague to define the *customer* and they will probably say 'Someone who buys from us', ie: the external customer.

What about internal customers? Colleagues, other departments, branches, suppliers? They are equally as important and deserve to have their problems and complaints taken seriously.

External customers sense if there is a good working atmosphere, a co-ordinated approach to customer service, teamwork and high morale.

It gives them confidence to stay with you.

# PASSING BLAME

Why is it that when customers blame us for something going wrong we are quick to blame others, especially in big organisations.

'We passed the order to Stores weeks ago. I don't know what they have done with it.' (You know very well it's still in your in-tray!)

Customers see through these feeble excuses and are not impressed!

## Why do this?

- Stores are always making mistakes; attributing one more to them won't make any difference
- There's a particular person in Stores you don't like
- No one will find out whether they are to blame are not
- They have blamed your department often enough
- They always beat your staff at the annual bowling challenge

INTERNAL COMPLAINTS

# TWO WAY PROCESS

Lack of communication between departments is often cited as the reason for poor working relationships. *They never tell us anything* is a frequent cry.

Communication is a **two way process**. The most efficient of systems will not be effective if people don't read their messages, look at the noticeboards, log on to their computers, check their voice mail or pay attention at meetings.

Getting people to sign memos only provides proof of receipt, not of having read them. They need to **want** to know what's going on.

Low morale and a critical and suspicious environment will prompt employees to see customers as a nuisance and not the lifeblood of the business.

Every employee needs to appreciate that they contribute to customer satisfaction even if they are working behind the scenes, eg: maintenance, cleaning, refuse collection, etc. They deserve to be kept informed!

# COMPANY CULTURE

Some departments pride themselves on being the most efficient, the best organised, the most responsive, and expect others to live up to their standards and follow their procedures. This can foster resentment and lead to a refusal to co-operate. Frustration and conflict can cause bad feeling and a desire to sabotage. This often happens when an organisation has no clear vision or has not communicated one to the staff. Poor leadership or managers with their own agendas are other contributory factors.

Working in isolation, split site or satellite offices often result in an autonomous management with a workforce who want to do their 'own thing'.

This has a negative effect on customer satisfaction. Customers become the victims of internal politics. What's it got to do with them?

# INSECURITY

Another cause of internal conflict is insecurity: downsizing, management restructuring, fast-talking business consultants, threats of job loss, short term contracts, all might trigger a loss of pride in the job and a *couldn't care less* attitude. Customers become anxious and take their business elsewhere.

Insecurity manifests itself in a number of behaviours:

- Gossip and back-stabbing
- Shifting blame
- Anger, depression
- Increase in absences due to stress
- Constant moaning and whinging
- Negative thinking

In this environment it is likely that customer complaints will increase. It is essential to keep the customer at the centre of everything you do, no matter what is going on behind the scenes. **Without customers you don't have a job**.

## INTERNAL COMPLAINTS

# TAKING ACTION

Managers need to be very observant. Early identification of problems is the key to a successful solution.

Look out for:
- Deadlines not met
- Increase in illness
- Poor quality work
- Atmospheres
- Arguments

Action:
- Ask questions in a confidential manner
- Reassure, calm fears
- Praise, encourage
- Don't blame or challenge
- Involve people
- Motivate, reward

# MULTI-SKILLING & INTERDEPARTMENTAL WORKING

Conflict also arises through ignorance. Giving people the opportunity to learn about the work of others and equipping them with new skills, helps dispel fears, boost confidence and motivate. It also takes people out of their enclosed worlds of Accounts or the Postroom and gives them the bigger picture.

Many complaints arise because staff feel they are expected to do a job without any training. Allowing them to attend courses out of the workplace is very beneficial. It gives them the opportunity to network with others, revitalise their ideas and acquire new skills. Hopefully they'll come back and think, 'It's not such a bad place after all'.

In any business, we are all customers of each other. Unless we get the internal customer service right it won't extend naturally to external customers.

How can you do this?

- Have a positive attitude to your own work and that of your colleagues
- Help out when necessary
- Remember you are all working for a common aim: **customer satisfaction**

# TEAM BUILDING

It isn't necessary to take the workforce abseiling in North Wales to 'bond', build trust or foster better working relationships.

Time away from the desk or shop floor to discuss issues in small groups, social evenings and interdepartmental activities can be just as effective.

Everyone needs to understand their own worth and value to the company.

High self-esteem = reduction in conflict = better customer relations = more profitable business.

NOTES

# BUILDING CUSTOMER LOYALTY

# COMPLAINTS INTO COMPLIMENTS

It's a mistake to think that because a customer has expressed dissatisfaction with your product or service they will not come back to you.

They won't return if you handle the situation badly. However, some of your most vociferous complainers could become your most loyal customers because you handled the situation well and treated them with respect.

This means recognising some essential traits:

- Customers want to be liked
- They want attention
- They want to be appreciated and recognised
- They want to be understood

# LOSING CUSTOMERS

Why do businesses lose customers?

A survey with which you may be familiar asked customers why they left businesses. They gave these reasons:

- Developed a good relationship with another supplier   5%
- Cheaper products elsewhere   9%
- Unhappy with service/product   15%
- Because of poor attitude of supplier   **68%**
- Moved away   3%

# TREAT LIKE ROYALTY

It's easy to win new business but we should nurture
existing customers and try to minimise problems
and inconvenience.

It's a good idea to:

- Make regular visits or calls – spotting trouble
  early on can help prevent it
- Reply to calls/queries as soon as possible
- Talk to your customers – find out about them
- Offer them occasional treats – free tickets,
  quality wine
- Keep them well informed

Treating them like *royalty* helps to build *loyalty*.

# SOLVING PROBLEMS

Suppose they are difficult.

Few people are truly difficult. In any case it is important to make a distinction between difficult people and difficult behaviour, which is often a result of non-cooperation on your part.

- Focus on the problem not on them
- Show interest – bring out their likeable side
- Put yourself in their shoes
- Be personal – use their name if that's what they would like
- Appeal to their better nature, 'As a parent of small children you … '
- Cultivate their goodwill

# SAYING THANK YOU

Let your customers know you appreciate them. Find little ways to thank them for their custom, especially when they are not expecting it. This is a great way to attract compliments, especially after sorting out a difficult problem.

- A simple but sincere thank you card – personalised
- Gift vouchers
- Cards at Christmas or other appropriate festivals – Diwali, Hanukah, Eid
- VIP days for special events, launches, dinners
- Social gatherings for key clients

Loyalty cards are very popular now with many organisations. Discounts, bonus points, free samples all help to make your business stand out.

## COMPLIMENTS & COMMENTS

Why do we find it difficult to accept compliments?

Is it because:-

- We don't have enough faith or pride in our product?
- We think it's probably a back-handed complaint?
- We don't trust people?
- We don't know how to react? *(How about thank you?!)*

Compliments tell us what we are doing right and give a boost to our morale. If we allow it they bring us pleasure.

Some customers just mutter a comment because that's how they are. They don't really want you to take them up on it. It's a good idea though to take note of what they say and if appropriate ask, 'Is everything okay?'.

# RELATIONSHIP MARKETING

Relationship marketing might be a new buzz word but it's here to stay. It's all about looking at your customers and your relationship with them in a new light. Rather than develop a product or service and market it to the customers, relationship marketeers think about what the customers want and adapt their product accordingly.

It's about *customisation* to meet the needs of the individual.

Relationship marketing is based on getting **feedback** and using it to develop and improve your service. Earlier it was suggested that companies make it as easy as possible for customers to complain. In relationship marketing, feedback is sought **before** a complaint occurs. This helps to:

- Identify potential problem areas before the customer does
- Customise

For many companies it has become common practice to encourage customers to provide such information via the website.

You need good quality of information if you are to have a two way relationship with your customer.

# CUSTOMER EXPECTATIONS

**Have today's customers changed?**

- They are more demanding
- Have higher expectations
- Have a more pressurised lifestyle
- Want everything but don't necessarily want to pay for it
- Are less tolerant
- Want more for their money, time and effort
- Are much more aware of their rights – influenced by consumer rights programmes
- Are driven by customer service issues in their own workplace
- Are more likely to seek recommendation from friends and colleagues than rely on advertising
- Are driven by new technology – particularly the internet

# AND FINALLY

**Some key lessons on keeping abreast of customer needs and minimising complaints:**

- Use as much of the available technology as possible – make it work for the customer
- Focus on customers as individuals
- Listen and act on what they say
- Increase the value of each customer – especially in the long term
- Welcome complaints

Some famous words to remember:

**Rule No 1 - The customer is always right**
**Rule No 2 - If you find the customer is wrong, return to Rule 1!**

# BIBLIOGRAPHY

Thomas A. Harris, *I'm OK – You're OK,* Arrow Books

Ros Jay, *Smart Customers,* Capstone Publishing

Tony Newby and Sean McManus, *The Customer Service Pocketbook,*
Management Pocketbooks

# THE MANAGEMENT POCKETBOOK SERIES

## Pocketbooks

Appraisals
Assertiveness
Balance Sheet
Business Planning
Business Writing
Call Centre Customer Care
Career Transition
Challengers
Coaching
Communicator's
Competencies
Controlling Absenteeism
Creative Manager's
C.R.M.
Cross-cultural Business
Cultural Gaffes
Customer Service
Decision-making
Developing People
Discipline
Diversity
E-commerce
Emotional Intelligence
Employment Law
Empowerment

Energy and Well-being
Facilitator's
Flexible Workplace
Handling Complaints
Icebreakers
Impact & Presence
Improving Efficiency
Improving Profitability
Induction
Influencing
International Trade
Interviewer's
I.T. Trainer's
Key Account Manager's
Leadership
Learner's
Manager's
Managing Budgets
Managing Cashflow
Managing Change
Managing Recruitment
Managing Upwards
Managing Your Appraisal
Marketing
Meetings

Mentoring
Motivation
Negotiator's
Networking
NLP
Openers & Closers
People Manager's
Performance Management
Personal Success
Positive Mental Attitude
Presentations
Problem Behaviour
Problem Solving
Project Management
Quality
Resolving Conflict
Sales Excellence
Salesperson's
Self-managed Development
Starting In Management
Strategy
Stress
Succeeding at Interviews
Teambuilding Activities
Teamworking

Telephone Skills
Telesales
Thinker's
Time Management
Trainer Standards
Trainer's
Training Evaluation
Training Needs Analysis
Virtual Teams
Vocal Skills

## Pocketsquares

Great Training Robbery
Hook Your Audience

## Pocketfiles

Trainer's Blue Pocketfile of
Ready-to-use Activities

Trainer's Green Pocketfile of
Ready-to-use Activities

Trainer's Red Pocketfile of
Ready-to-use Activities

27.2.06

# ORDER FORM

**Your details**

Name _____

Position _____

Company _____

Address _____

_____

Telephone _____

Fax _____

E-mail _____

VAT No. (EC companies) _____

Your Order Ref _____

**Please send me:**

| | No. copies |
| --- | --- |
| The Handling Complaints Pocketbook | ☐ |
| The _____ Pocketbook | ☐ |
| The _____ Pocketbook | ☐ |
| The _____ Pocketbook | ☐ |
| The _____ Pocketbook | ☐ |

*Order by Post*

**MANAGEMENT POCKETBOOKS LTD**

LAUREL HOUSE, STATION APPROACH,
ALRESFORD, HAMPSHIRE SO24 9JH  UK

*Order by Phone, Fax or Internet*

Telephone: +44 (0)1962 735573
Facsimile:  +44 (0)1962 733637
E-mail: sales@pocketbook.co.uk
Web: www.pocketbook.co.uk

**MANAGEMENT POCKETBOOKS**

## About the Author

**Angelena Boden  BA, M.Soc.Sc., PGCE**
Angelena is a freelance trainer in customer service, language and culture, and people behaviour. This is her fourth Pocketbook and one she feels is very much needed in business today.

"Customers today are very demanding. TV programmes like Watchdog have made people more aware of their rights. Dealing with complaints can be very rewarding. It can be the ultimate test of professionalism."

Angelena runs a range of one day seminar programmes: complaint handling; how to deal with difficult people; coping in a crisis; advanced communication for difficult situations. She also presents tailor-made courses for industry.

**Contact**
Angelena's contact details are:
E-mail: peoplecomefirst@hotmail.com
www.peoplecomefirst.org.uk